Cybercriminals

WIL MARA

Children's Press®
An Imprint of Scholastic Inc.

Content Consultant
Albert E. Scherr, JD
Chair, International Criminal Law and Justice Programs
University of New Hampshire School of Law
Concord, New Hampshire

Library of Congress Cataloging-in-Publication Data
Mara, Wil.
 Cybercriminals / Wil Mara.
   pages cm. — (A true book)
 Includes bibliographical references and index.
 ISBN 978-0-531-21465-7 (library binding) — ISBN 978-0-531-22078-8 (pbk.)
 1. Computer crimes. 2. Internet—Safety measures. I. Title.
 HV6773.M366 2016
 364.16'8—dc23   2015023742

Front cover: A man commits cybercrime using a tablet computer

Back cover: A man is arrested

Find the Truth!

Everything you are about to read is true *except* for one of the sentences on this page.

Which one is **TRUE**?

T or F   Most cybercriminals are over the age of 40.

T or F   Most cybercriminals are male.

Find the answers in this book.

Contents

1 In the Shadows

What exactly is a cybercrime?..................7

2 New Crimes, New Methods

What are the different types of cybercrimes? 11

THE BIG TRUTH!

On the Defense

How do people protect themselves
and their data? 22

3 People Without Faces

What characteristics do hackers and
other online criminals share? 25

Virus Alert!

Warning! Threat detected!

A malicious item has been detected!

Security programs scan a computer for any viruses or other malware.

4 The Tools of the Trade

How are cybercrimes committed?. **33**

5 Fighting Back

How have authorities tried to limit computer and Internet crime?. **39**

True Statistics. **44**

Resources **45**

Important Words. **46**

Index **47**

About the Author. **48**

People submitted nearly 270,000 complaints of cybercrime to the Federal Bureau of Investigation in 2014.

Anyone who uses a computer may become a victim of cybercrime.

CHAPTER 1

In the Shadows

Since the introduction of the personal computer in 1974 and the World Wide Web in 1991, the digital age has thoroughly changed society. Today, computers can do so much so quickly. They help with homework and deliver the latest news and sports scores. They provide entertainment and keep people in touch. But they have also led to cybercrime. Using computers, cybercriminals can hide in the shadows while committing dangerous and costly crimes.

Even when we stop a cybercrime, we don't always identify the person behind it.

Computer Crimes

A cybercrime is any act intended to harm an individual or group with the aid of a computer. The computer could be a laptop, desktop, tablet, or even a smartphone. In most cases, the crime also involves the Internet. Cybercrime is becoming one of the costliest types of crime in the world. Read on to learn about modern thieves called cybercriminals, what's being done to protect people from them, and what you can do to protect yourself!

Big businesses, with a lot of sensitive data stored on large servers, are often the targets of cybercrime.

Jennifer works hard to be a safe and responsible computer user.

Jennifer, Part 1—A Really Good Kid

Jennifer Z. is 16 years old. She spends about an hour or so each day on her laptop at home. When she chats with friends online, she uses the screen name "Jenny Zee." Her computer has all the normal protective **software**. She doesn't open e-mails from addresses she doesn't recognize, doesn't download things without permission, and doesn't visit any Web sites she shouldn't. All in all, she's a really good kid when it comes to using her computer.

CHAPTER 2

New Crimes, New Methods

It is really quite remarkable how many different types of crimes can be carried out on one's laptop, tablet, or cellphone. Some cybercrimes are completely new. They simply could not exist without computers. Other cybercrimes are the same type of crimes people committed long before computers. The difference is that computers have opened new opportunities and methods to these criminals.

Some cybercriminals specifically target smartphones.

Virus Alert!

Warning! Threat detected!
A malicious item has been detected!

Special programs on a computer warn a user when they detect malware.

High-Tech Abilities

Malware such as **viruses** are among the new types of hostile and intrusive software made possible by computers. Cybercriminals intentionally nestle malware into a computer system to cause damage. The malware may be relatively harmless. For example, your computer shuts down one time, just to annoy you. Malware can also be much more serious. Some might erase huge amounts of data or corrupt a computer code so a device no longer functions properly.

Hacking allows criminals to break through security systems to access another computer's data. Hackers can work anonymously without people knowing who they are. This makes them difficult to catch.

These new, high-tech abilities have opened new doors for criminals. From theft to harassment, malware and hacking have shaped new methods and opportunities for even the oldest of crimes.

Hackers may steal a victim's passwords to access protected data.

Stealing Money

Before computers, a thief might break into a home or steal someone's wallet. Now, a criminal just needs a computer. They can hack into a bank's system and remove money from one account or add money to another. Thieves can also charge goods and services to a victim's credit card or steal other people's identities to claim their money. A thief can even force someone to hand over money through threats.

Some cybercriminals demand payment through Bitcoin, a method of anonymous online payment.

Using credit cards to make online purchases puts people at risk of having their card numbers stolen.

Hackers might steal details about a project that a company has spent years developing.

Stealing Knowledge

The theft of valuable information is becoming popular in the world of cybercrime. Hackers can access and use private information such as passwords or identification numbers of any ordinary person. Companies sometimes steal information on one another's new products. Individuals or groups may steal knowledge to share it with the public. WikiLeaks is one example. This Web site published secret materials that often came from hackers or sources inside governments or similar organizations.

A File or Two

In recent decades, it has become common for companies to sell books, movies, games, software, music, and other **copyrighted** materials as computer files. There are now new possibilities for stealing these materials. People can illegally download files for free if others have made them available. They may watch movies, play games, or listen to music without paying. Illegal downloading can take place across the world. For example, a hacker in Sweden may download a favorite band's new album from a computer in Mexico.

Music is one of the most common copyrighted materials to be illegally downloaded.

From Fortune to Prison

The year 2013 saw one of history's biggest cybercrimes. Authorities arrested five men for hacking into the systems of some of the world's largest companies. These included JCPenney, JetBlue, and Visa. The hackers stole sensitive customer information and sold it to other people. Each group member had a specialized task. For example, one person may have hacked through the security systems, another collected the data, and a third sold that data. Authorities believe the crimes cost the companies more than $300 million combined.

Harassment can cause serious damage to a person's emotional health.

Harassment

Every day, thousands of people are abused because of their gender, background, beliefs, sexual orientation, appearance, and so on. Bullying has happened in person for generations. Today, bullies have found new outlets through text messages, chat rooms, and e-mail. Social media sites such as Twitter and Facebook are also bullying tools. In many countries, it is illegal to personally attack someone over the Internet. Such attacks are among the world's most common cybercrimes.

Terrorist Activity

Terrorists disrupt daily life for political reasons by creating fear. Cyberterrorists may hack into a government's computer systems and damage or steal information. They could also spread a rumor on the Internet. For example, terrorists hacked into the Twitter account of Associated Press, a news agency, in 2013. Pretending to be the organization, they tweeted that the White House was attacked. People panicked, and U.S. financial markets dipped before the truth came out.

Employees at the U.S. National Cybersecurity and Communications Integration Center work to protect the government from cyberterrorism and other computer crimes.

Computers play an important role in a lot of military activity. Disrupting these computer systems can cause major problems where national security is concerned—and that, in turn, can risk serious loss of life.

Open Warfare

War has traditionally taken place through soldiers, tanks, planes, and battlefields. However, cyberwarfare is rapidly becoming the wave of the future. A nation can cause serious damage by penetrating an enemy's computer systems. For example, a program may provide a government's hacker with access to an enemy country's nuclear bombs. This could allow the hacker's government to control where, when, and if the bombs are used.

Jennifer, Part 2—Something Very Wrong

It's a typical Tuesday night. Jennifer did her homework after dinner and watched TV. She's now online chatting with some friends through a Web site designed for teens. They're all talking about a band's upcoming album. Then a new person joins the conversation. Jennifer doesn't recognize the screen name. The person starts off friendly enough, but then the comments turn very personal. In front of her friends, Jen is told how nice she looks in certain outfits. When Jen asks who he or she is, the person doesn't answer.

Be careful what information you share online, especially if you're not sure whom you're talking to.

On the Defense

You have many ways to defend yourself against cyberattacks. Even in the comfort of your own home, you can make your devices and your most valuable data almost impossible to access.

Do not expose all your files to the Internet.
Detachable hard drives help keep important files safe. Attach these drives to your computer only when you want to work on any files they contain.

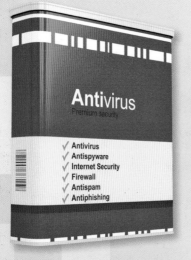

Always update your protective software.
Update your antivirus and other protective software so it can recognize and eliminate these new threats.

Antivirus
Premium security
✓ Antivirus
✓ Antispyware
✓ Internet Security
✓ Firewall
✓ Antispam
✓ Antiphishing

Never open e-mails from an address you don't recognize.
One of the easiest ways for a cybercriminal to gain access to your computer is through e-mail. They often come with an enticing subject line, such as "Your best friend is trying to reach you!" or "You just won a hundred dollars." Never open such e-mails.

Only download software and other files from a reliable and trusted source.
If Microsoft asks you to download Windows updates, that's fine. Recklessly downloading materials from unfamiliar sites, however, is not good. You may end up downloading a virus.

Back up important data often.
Back up important data every two or three days. There are many programs that do this for you. Ideally, back up your important data to a detachable drive, such as a flash drive, and then put it in a safe place.

People Without Faces

The problem with catching cybercriminals is that law enforcement can't see them. One of the fundamental elements of cybercrime is anonymity. Yet authorities have recognized some common traits among these criminals. Many of them are men between the ages of 14 and 40. They often are smart, introverted (not particularly social), independent, and controlling. They also tend to be passionate about their beliefs and dislike rules and laws.

Hackers and other cybercriminals take advantage of the fact that computers help them stay anonymous.

Why Do They Do It?

One of the most common reasons people commit cybercrime is to steal money. Political beliefs are another driving factor. People often become very passionate about their views. They may find the computer a useful instrument for forcing their ideas on others. Another motive is anger. Someone feeling wronged or outraged might use cybercrime to seek revenge on someone else.

Many cybercriminals focus on making money—but some have other motives.

Children are among the individuals most often targeted in cybercrime.

Amusement is another possible reason. Some people just get a kick out of causing trouble. Unfortunately, this attitude has caused a great deal of loss and pain for otherwise law-abiding people.

Another type of cybercriminal goes online to set up inappropriate or dangerous conversations or meetings with strangers. Often, these strangers are children. Such **online predators** may pretend to be older, younger, or another gender online to gain a person's trust.

A Range of Cybercriminals

One of the most common types of hacker is known as a black hat hacker. These people work for personal gain or to cause trouble. Examples include the men who hacked into Visa and other companies in 2013. Gray hat hackers just hack for the challenge. They might break through a Web site's security, but not steal or damage any data.

Many white hat and other professional hackers started out as gray or black hat hackers.

Hacktivists may commit cybercrimes to bring attention and support to political movements.

White hat hackers fall into a kind of "good guy" category. They often work for companies and governments. They have permission from their employers to try to break through security systems and expose flaws to be repaired. Government hackers may also break into enemy governments' computers to spy and discover secrets.

Then there are hacktivists. These are people who hack computers to further their political or philosophical views.

Jennifer, Part 3—Who Could It Be?

The next day, Jen becomes really worried. The unknown person has commented again about her looks. The sender knew what she had worn to school and that her hair had been in a ponytail. Besides that, the sender has asked questions that seem really inappropriate. Why does this person want to know her father's job? At first, she thinks it's one of the boys in her class. But none of her classmates seem like they'd do this.

Sometimes a hacker can be an ordinary student in an ordinary school—including yours.

Skill Set

Cybercrime cannot really be called a profession. However, cybercriminals do need certain skills to commit their crimes. First of all, hackers are very good with a computer. They keep up on the latest technology. They also have advanced programming skills. They need to understand the design and structure of protection programs that they encounter. They also use their programming skills to create their own hacking applications. All these specialized abilities make hackers very good at controlling technology.

A talented hacker knows exactly what he or she needs to build the perfect computer.

CHAPTER 4

The Tools of the Trade

How do cybercriminals carry out their purpose? First and foremost, they need a computer with all the necessary **hardware** and software. Some hackers build their own computers from the ground up, carefully choosing each piece of the system. Very often it will be the best that is currently available. They may also go with an **operating system** that is easier to personalize, such as Linux.

Building your own computer is not as difficult as you might think.

Choosing Between Computers

A laptop's mobility is useful when intimidating or harassing someone. A smartphone or tablet could work, too. Wireless Internet access is free in countless different places, and many

A laptop allows a cybercriminal to work from any place that has Internet access.

phones can connect from almost anywhere. A harasser may easily find a place to send messages from and then disappear. Some cybercriminals, however, stay home, and a standard desktop computer is enough for them. Someone committing a cybercrime from work or school may use whatever computer is available.

Software

With an adaptable operating system such as Linux, a cybercriminal can adjust his or her computer to suit a particular purpose. Other cybercriminals may use programs we all use every day, including Microsoft Windows. On top of whatever operating system they use, cybercriminals also use specialized applications. These modern criminals either design these programs themselves or download them from the Internet. For example, there are programs specifically designed to help someone surf the Internet anonymously.

Some cybercriminals are talented programmers.

Many companies and organizations use special scanning software to find and fix vulnerabilities in their own system. These programs are designed to help people keep their systems closed to cybercrime. Cybercriminals, however, use these programs for their own purposes. They might scan a system, find its weaknesses, and then use those openings to access, damage, or steal data.

Scanners can pinpoint a computer system's weakest areas.

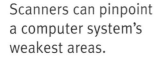

Detectives visited Jennifer's house to discuss the messages she received.

Jennifer, Part 4—The Law

Jen tells her parents about the creepy messages. Her parents tell the police. The next day, two cybercrime detectives visit their home and run tests from Jen's computer. They've seen similar comments before in town. They also recognize the person's language, including favored words and repeated misspellings. It's someone they've been tracking for weeks. The sender uses illegal software that blocks his or her exact location, though. This makes it harder to know where he or she is.

There are women hackers, as well as men, but they are the minority where hacking is concerned.

CHAPTER 5

Fighting Back

As long as there are criminals, there will be people who fight them. There's not much anyone can do to *predict* attacks. There are antivirus programs and **firewalls**, however, designed to halt suspicious activity. Files and folders can be password protected. Many companies hire specialists to probe their networks for vulnerabilities. There are also experts in the growing field of **intent recognition**. These experts identify patterns in online behavior that suggest dangerous or illegal activity.

Fighting cybercrime has become a major focus of law enforcement.

No Fooling

Many people try to fool cybercriminals. For example, some companies hide harmless decoy data where a hacker might expect to find sensitive information. This keeps the hacker away from any real data. Security firms design malware-type programs that mine information from the *criminal's* machine. This makes it easier to catch the criminals. Law enforcement members sometimes pretend to be a friend and try to set up a meeting with the criminal. Some cybercriminals fall for it and get caught!

Timeline of Cybercrime

1991
The World Wide Web is made available to the public.

1975
The first personal computers are sold to the public.

1988
Cybercriminals release the first computer virus on private networks.

Legal Action

Cybercrime is relatively new. So are the many laws against it. One of the most important in the United States is the 1986 Computer Fraud and Abuse Act. It legally defines what qualifies as a computer crime and what types of computers and data are protected. Another is the 1998 Identity Theft and Assumption Deterrence Act. It outlaws using another person's identity to conduct illegal actions online. This discourages hackers who use identity theft to steal money or commit other crimes.

2013

Five hackers steal customer information from major companies such as JCPenney, JetBlue, and Visa.

2006

Hackers break into the National Aeronautics and Space Administration (NASA) networks.

Depending on the crime, a cybercriminal might spend several years in prison.

There are also laws that establish punishments for cybercrimes. Heavier punishments include fines of hundreds of thousands of dollars and 15- to 20-year prison sentences. One problem in enforcing these laws, however, is that cybercriminals may be in one country while their victims are in another. Because each country has its own separate legal system, the countries must cooperate before the criminal can be punished. Governments around the world are working on new international agreements to solve this problem.

Jennifer, Part 5—Surprise

The police decided to try luring Jennifer's online predator into the open. The criminal knew what Jennifer looked like, so he or she probably lived in the same town. The police pretended to be Jennifer and talked to the person about meeting. The person asked to meet behind a supermarket one night. Sure enough, there he was—and so were the police. It turned out he was a man in his thirties who lived down the street. He had been harassing quite a few girls in the neighborhood. Not anymore! ★

Police successfully found and arrested the man who had been harassing Jennifer.

True Statistics

Countries with the most incidents of cybercrime: The United States, China, and Germany

Most common targets of cybercrime: Large industries, governments, and educational institutions

Most common forms of cybercrime: Viruses and botnets (a system of computers all infected with a virus that gives an outside user control)

Most common reasons people commit cybercrimes: Theft (money, information), hacktivism, spying

Annual cost of cybercrime worldwide: About $450 billion

Number of new cybercrime victims each day: About 1 million

Number of cybercrimes committed every second: 12

Percentage of cybercrimes organized and committed by criminal groups: 80

Did you find the truth?

F Most cybercriminals are over the age of 40.

T Most cybercriminals are male.

Resources

Books

Cornwall, Phyllis. *Online Etiquette and Safety*. North Mankato MN: Cherry Lake, 2013.

Latta, Sara. *Cybercrime: Data Trails DO Tell Tales*. Berkeley Heights, NJ: Enslow, 2012.

McAneney, Caitie. *Online Safety*. New York: PowerKids Press, 2015.

Truesdell, Ann. *How to Handle Cyberbullies*. Ann Arbor, MI: Cherry Lake, 2014.

Visit this Scholastic Web site for more information on cybercriminals:
★ www.factsfornow.scholastic.com
Enter the keyword **Cybercriminals**

Important Words

antivirus (an-ti-VYE-ruhs) — designed to protect computers from viruses

copyrighted (KAH-pee-rite-id) — legally owned and controlled

firewalls (FIRE-wawlz) — software designed to control access to a computer to protect it from outside attacks

hacking (HAK-ing) — breaking into a computer system to secretly change it or get information from it without permission

hardware (HARD-wair) — computer equipment

intent recognition (in-TENT rek-uhg-NISH-uhn) — the practice of trying to predict what a person wants to accomplish through their online activity

online predators (AHN-line PRED-uh-turz) — people who use the Internet to harass or otherwise harm children

operating system (AH-puh-rate-ing SIS-tuhm) — the software in a computer that supports all the programs that run on it

software (SAWFT-wair) — computer programs that control the workings of equipment, or hardware

viruses (VYE-ruhs-iz) — computer programs that produce many copies of themselves and are designed to destroy a computer system or damage data

Index

Page numbers in **bold** indicate illustrations.

anonymity, 13, 14, **24**, 25, 35, 37
antivirus software, **22**–23, 39
arrests, 17, **42**, **43**

backups, **23**
banks, 14, **17**, 28, **41**
bullying, **18**

cellphones, 11
children, **27**
Computer Fraud and Abuse Act (1986), 41
computers, **6**, 7, 8, 11, **20**, **24**, **32**, 33, **34**, **40**, 41
copyrighted materials, **16**
credit cards, **14**, **17**, 28

decoy data, 40
downloads, 9, 16, **23**, 35

e-mail, 9, 18, 23

firewalls, 39

gray hat hackers, 28

hacktivists, **29**
hard drives, **22**
harrassment, 18, 21, 30, 34, 37, **43**

identity theft, 14, 41
Identity Theft and Assumption Deterrence Act (1998), 41
information, **15**, 17, 19, **21**, 40, **41**
intent recognition, 39

laptops, 8, 11, **34**

law enforcement, 25, **37**, 40, **43**
laws, 18, 25, 41–42

malware, **12**, 13, 22, 40
money, 14, **26**, 41
motivation, **26**–27

online predators, 21, 27, 30, 37, **43**
operating systems, 33, 35

passwords, **13**, 15, 39
political beliefs, 19, 26, **29**
punishments, **42**

safety, **9**, **22–23**
scanning software, **36**
screen names, 9, 21
skills, 31, **32**, 33, **35**, 36
smartphones, 8, **10**, 11, 34
social media, 18, 19
software, 9, **12**, 16, **22**–23, 31, 33, **35**, 36, 37, 39, 40

tablet computers, 8, 11, 34
targets, **8**, **10**, 11, **18**, 19, **20**, **27**, 29
terrorism, **19**
threats, 14, 19
timeline, **40–41**
traits, 25

viruses, 12, **22**–23, 39, 40

Web sites, 9, 15, 21, 29
white hat hackers, **28**
WikiLeaks, 15, 29

About the Author

Wil Mara is the award-winning, bestselling author of more than 140 books, many of which are educational titles for young readers. Over the years, he has consulted with agents in both the FBI and the CIA concerning cybercrime, mostly in the course of research for his novels for adult readers. He has also been the editor for numerous cybersecurity titles for textbook publisher Prentice Hall.

[5]